THE
GETTYSBURG ADDRESS

in Translation

What It Really Means

by Kay Melchisedech Olson

Consultant:
Erin I. Bishop, PhD, Director of Education
Abraham Lincoln Presidential Library and Museum
Springfield, Illinois

Capstone
press

Mankato, Minnesota

Fact Finders is published by Capstone Press,
151 Good Counsel Drive, P.O. Box 669, Mankato, Minnesota 56002.
www.capstonepress.com

Library of Congress Cataloging-in-Publication Data
Olson, Kay Melchisedech.
    The Gettysburg Address in translation: what it really means / by Kay Melchisedech Olson.
    p. cm. — (Fact finders. Kids' translations)
    Summary: "Presents the full text of the Gettysburg Address in both its original version and in a translated
version using everyday language. Describes the events that led to Lincoln's famous speech and its significance
through history" — Provided by publisher.
    Includes bibliographical references and index.
    ISBN-13: 978-1-4296-1930-1 (hardcover)
    ISBN-10: 1-4296-1930-9 (hardcover)
    ISBN-13: 978-1-4296-2845-7 (softcover pbk.)
    ISBN-10: 1-4296-2845-6 (softcover pbk.)
    1. Lincoln, Abraham, 1809–1865. Gettysburg address — Juvenile literature. I. Title.
E475.55.O46 2009
973.7092 — dc22
                    2007051301

Editorial Credits

Megan Schoeneberger, editor; Gene Bentdahl, set designer and illustrator; Wanda Winch,
    photo researcher

Photo Credits

Abraham Lincoln, Draft of the Gettysburg Address: Nicolay Copy, November 1863; Series 3, General Correspondence,
    1837–1897; The Abraham Lincoln Papers at the Library of Congress, Manuscript Division (Washington, D. C.:
    American Memory Project, [2000-02]), 4 (right), 6 , 7 (top), 8 (right), 20 (right)
Capstone Press/Karon Dubke, cover, 9 (left), 17, 28
The Century Atlas of the World, Published by The Century Co., New York, 1900, Cultural Resources, Inc., 11
Corbis Royalty-Free, 16, 22, 23
Courtesy of the Adams County Historical Society, Gettysburg, PA, 12
David Wills to Abraham Lincoln, Monday, November 02, 1863; Series 1, General Correspondence, 1833-1916; The
    Abraham Lincoln Papers at the Library of Congress, Manuscript Division (Washington, D. C.: American Memory
    Project, [2000-02]), 21(bottom)
Getty Images Inc./Hulton Archive, 8 (left); Time Life Pictures/Eliot Elisofon, 10
James P. Rowan, 18
Library of Congress, cover (Abraham Lincoln), 4 (left), 5, 7 (bottom), 13, 15, 19
National Archives and Records Administration, 9 (right)
North Wind Picture Archives, 14, 20 (left)
PictureHistory, 21 (top)
Shutterstock/K.L. Kohn, 25

Editor's Notes:
This book uses the Bancroft copy of the Gettysburg Address as the primary source.
Essential content terms are **bold** and are defined at the bottom of the page where they first appear.

1 2 3 4 5 6 13 12 11 10 09 08

Table of Contents

CHAPTER 1

The Gettysburg Address
WHAT IT IS

Crowds of people head to the dedication ceremony at the Soldiers' National Cemetery in Gettysburg on November 19, 1863.

portrait of Abraham Lincoln
dated November 8, 1863

On November 19, 1863, about 15,000 people gathered in Gettysburg, Pennsylvania. They were there to **dedicate** a national cemetery. The cemetery was for soldiers who had died in the Battle of Gettysburg.

The **Civil War** was in its third year. States from the North, or Union, were fighting states from the South. The Battle of Gettysburg was the first battle fought on Union ground. Several thousand soldiers died on both sides.

The dedication ceremony included music, prayers, and a two-hour speech by Edward Everett, a famous speaker. Near the end of the program, President Abraham Lincoln stood to say a few words.

dedicate — to devote something to a special purpose

civil war — a war between people who all live in the same country

The audience was silent, straining to hear the president's words. In three short minutes, Lincoln's speech was finished. He sat down. The photographer didn't even have time to take a picture. Lincoln had spoken only a few hundred words. But those few words became one of the most famous speeches ever given in the United States.

Today, there are five known copies of Lincoln's Gettysburg Address written in his own handwriting. No one is sure which one he used at Gettysburg. Each of the five copies is slightly different. But they all contain the same message: the Union must be preserved.

Executive Mansion,

Washington,   , 186 .

Four score and seven years ago our fathers brought
forth, upon this continent, a new nation, conceived
in liberty, and dedicated to the proposition that
"all men are created equal"

Now we are engaged in a great civil
whether that nation, or any nation,
and so dedicated, can long endures.
on a great battle field of that wa
come to dedicate a portion of it, as
ing place for those who died her,
might live. This we may, in all propri
larger sense, we can not dedicat
consecrate— we can not hallow,
The brave men, living and de
hers, have hallowed it, for a
to add or detract.   the worl
her what we say here;
hers.

Did Lincoln Live in Gettysburg?

Lincoln's Gettysburg Address had nothing to do with where he lived. In this case, an address is a speech given before an audience. The program listed his speech as "Remarks from President A. Lincoln." It became known as the Gettysburg Address when newspapers reprinted Lincoln's words.

gateway to the Soldiers' National Cemetery at Gettysburg

What do Lincoln's words mean to you? Turn the page to take a closer look.

CHAPTER 2

The Gettysburg Address
WHAT IT MEANS

The Gettysburg Address

Four score and seven years ago our fathers brought forth, on this continent, a new nation, conceived in **Liberty**, and dedicated to the **proposition** that all men are created equal.

liberty — freedom

proposition — an offer or suggestion of an idea

8

1776

Lincoln was quoting the Declaration of Independence.

What?

Eighty-seven years ago, George Washington, Thomas Jefferson, Benjamin Franklin, and other men formed a new country, the United States of America. They believed that all people were free, and Americans should be free from **foreign control**. They based their new government on the idea that **all men are created equal**.

Until 1776, King George III in Great Britain ruled the American colonies. Colonists had no say in the government. They had to pay high taxes to King George III.

The Gettysburg Address Continued

Now we are **engaged** in a great civil war, testing whether that nation, or any nation so conceived, and so dedicated, can long **endure**. We are met on a great battle-field of that war. We have come to dedicate a portion of that field, as a final resting-place for those who here gave their lives, that this nation might live.

Who Is Buried at Gettysburg?

More than 3,000 soldiers are buried at Soldiers' National Cemetery. Most are Union soldiers. But more than 1,200 graves contain "Unknown Soldiers." These unidentified men could have been Confederate soldiers.

grave markers of the unknown soldiers at Gettysburg

endure — to last for a long time

engaged — taking part in

Today, **the states** are at war against each other. This **war** tests whether or not the United States of America can continue. We stand where a large Civil War battle was fought. We've come here to create a cemetery for **the men who fought and died** to keep our country united.

During the Civil War, Union states fought to keep the nation united and to end slavery. Confederate states fought to be a separate, independent nation.

More than 7,500 Union and Confederate soldiers died at Gettysburg.

The Civil War was fought between 23 Union states and 11 Confederate states.

The Gettysburg Address Continued

It is altogether fitting and proper that we should do this.

But, in a larger sense, we cannot dedicate — we cannot **consecrate** — we cannot **hallow** — this ground. The brave men, living and dead, who struggled here, have consecrated it far above our poor power to add or detract.

A Civilian Casualty

In his speech, Abraham Lincoln mentioned the brave men, both living and dead, who fought at Gettysburg. But not everyone who died at Gettysburg was a man or even a soldier.

Mary Virginia Wade, known as Jennie, was in the kitchen of her sister's house in Gettysburg. It was early morning on July 3, 1863. Jennie was probably busy making bread. Suddenly, a bullet from a Confederate gun ripped through the house. It struck Jennie in the back, killing her. Jennie Wade, at age 20, was the only civilian casualty of the Battle of Gettysburg.

consecrate — to bless or make holy

hallow — another word for consecrate

Jennie Wade

What?

It's only right that we honor **the men who died** here. After all, they gave their lives for our country. The **soldiers** have made this a holy ground. No matter what we do, we can never add to or take from their bravery.

Lincoln was careful not to praise Union soldiers or blame Confederate soldiers. Instead, he said that all the men who fought and died at Gettysburg should be honored.

Union soldier   Confederate soldier

The Gettysburg Address Continued

The world will little note, nor long remember what we say here, but it can never forget what they did here. It is for us the living, rather, to be dedicated here to the unfinished work which they who fought here have thus far so nobly advanced.

Confederate soldiers charged at Union soldiers during the Battle of Gettysburg.

People will soon forget about my speech.

But they will always remember the battle that was fought here. Those of us who are alive today have an important job to do. We must finish the work of the soldiers who died. They died to keep this country together. We must **continue that fight**.

Wrong! Lincoln's Gettysburg Address remains the most famous speech given by a U.S. president.

The Civil War lasted for another two years.

the Gettysburg battlefield

The Gettysburg Address Continued

It is rather for us to be here dedicated to the great task remaining before us — that from these honored dead we take increased **devotion** to that cause for which they here gave the last full measure of devotion — that we here highly **resolve** that these dead shall not have died in vain —

devotion — a strong interest

resolve — to decide that you will try hard to do something

What?

We must **keep this country together**. We owe a debt to the men who died here protecting this nation. It's up to us to make sure these men did not die for nothing.

Lincoln believed that the main purpose for the war was to keep the nation together.

Missed Opportunity

The Battle of Gettysburg could possibly have ended the Civil War. But Union generals failed to capture Confederate General Robert E. Lee and his men. They escaped from Pennsylvania. At the time of the Gettysburg Address, the war was not over. Lincoln needed the people's support to continue fighting it.

The Gettysburg Address Continued

that this nation, under God, shall have a new birth of freedom — and that government of the people, by the people, for the people, shall not **perish** from the earth.

Today, the Gettysburg battlefield is a National Military Park.

perish — to die

What?

Our country is a united nation here on earth. We have **fought for freedom** before and won. We formed our own government. We made our **own laws for our own people**. Now, we need a new kind of freedom. All citizens, **black** and white, must be free. That's the only way our country will survive.

In the Revolutionary War (1775–1783), American colonists fought for independence from Great Britain. They won.

Lincoln knew that the war was also about preserving the democracy started by the Founding Fathers.

About 180,000 free black soldiers fought for the Union in the Civil War.

CHAPTER 3

The Gettysburg Address
How It Came to Be

For three hot and horrible days in 1863, Union and Confederate soldiers battled in Gettysburg, Pennsylvania. The Civil War was in its third year. But this was the first time the Confederate army came north to fight on Union ground.

When the fighting ended on July 3, the Union seemed to be the winner. The Confederate army fled south. But both sides lost several thousand men.

David Wills

After the Battle

The people of Gettysburg were left with the bodies of dead soldiers rotting under the summer sun. Andrew Curtin, the governor of Pennsylvania, knew something had to be done. He hired David Wills, who lived in Gettysburg, to create a cemetery for the Union dead. By November 1863, the cemetery was ready. Wills invited Edward Everett to speak at the dedication. Wills also asked President Abraham Lincoln to address the crowd. The people of Gettysburg knew Lincoln received many invitations to give speeches. They never expected him to come.

David Wills' handwritten invitation to Lincoln

The Ceremony

People began crowding into the cemetery grounds early that cool November day. Some were governors of Union states. Some were Gettysburg citizens. Some were newspaper reporters. Many were soldiers still serving in the Union army.

It was hard to miss Lincoln in the parade to the cemetery. He rode on horseback, dressed in black. He sat tall in the saddle, holding the reins in his white-gloved hands. Around his tall hat was a mourning band. It was a symbol of his grief over the recent death of his young son Willie.

the only photo taken of Lincoln at Gettysburg

On this day, Lincoln felt weak and dizzy. He would later learn he had the start of a disease called smallpox. But his greatest concern was for his youngest son, Tad. Tad was sick back in Washington, D.C. Lincoln's wife, Mary, had begged her husband to stay home. But he had something important to say to the people at Gettysburg.

Just days after Lincoln took office, southern states withdrew from the Union. Not long after, the war between the North and South began. Thousands of men had died at Gettysburg, and the end of the war was not yet in sight.

Getting It Right

Lincoln wanted to get his message just right. He began writing his speech at the White House in Washington, D.C. The night before the dedication, Lincoln worked on it a little more.

Lincoln chose his words carefully. He knew that his most important job was to keep the country together. He wanted to keep the promise made in the Declaration of Independence that all men are created equal. He wanted to honor the dead. But he also wanted to inspire the living to continue to fight for the Union.

Lincoln was wrong in thinking that the world would forget what he said. In fact, Lincoln's words at Gettysburg have become more memorable than the battle itself.

What Was the Fighting about, Anyway?

It was states' rights – not slavery – that lit the fuse of the Civil War. Northern states believed the federal government should decide big issues for the entire country. Southern states believed the federal government was taking too much control from the states. They formed their own country, the Confederate States of America.

Lincoln's main goal was to keep the United States together. He did not believe the country could last if half the states had slaves and the other half did not. His words at Gettysburg echoed what he had said years earlier when asked about slavery. At that time, he said, "A house divided against itself cannot stand."

Abraham Lincoln is elected 16th President of the United States.

William Wallace "Willie" Lincoln, age 11, dies at the White House.

November 6, 1860

February 20, 1862

April 12, 1861

December 1860

January 1, 1863

South Carolina withdraws from the United States. Ten other states soon follow, forming the Confederate States of America (CSA or Confederacy).

Abraham Lincoln issues the Emancipation Proclamation. This document frees all slaves in Confederate states.

Confederate troops attack Fort Sumter, and the Civil War begins.

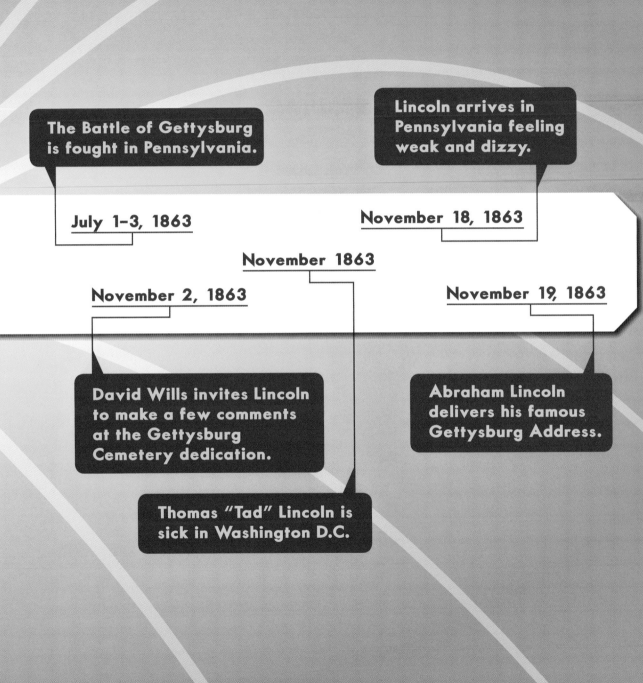

The Battle of Gettysburg is fought in Pennsylvania.

Lincoln arrives in Pennsylvania feeling weak and dizzy.

July 1–3, 1863

November 18, 1863

November 1863

November 2, 1863

November 19, 1863

David Wills invites Lincoln to make a few comments at the Gettysburg Cemetery dedication.

Abraham Lincoln delivers his famous Gettysburg Address.

Thomas "Tad" Lincoln is sick in Washington D.C.

Why Do I Care?

Top Five Reasons to Care about Lincoln's Gettysburg Address

5. More isn't necessarily better. Edward Everett spoke for more than two hours. Lincoln's well-chosen words took about three minutes to deliver.

4. Soldiers who give up their lives defending the country deserve honor and respect. Lincoln reminded people of this duty in his speech.

3. The United States was founded on the ideas of freedom and equality. Lincoln's speech reminded people that these principles are worth fighting for.

2. Practice makes perfect. Lincoln started writing his speech weeks before he gave it. He continued making improvements to get each word right.

1. Lincoln's Gettysburg Address brought people together by identifying a common goal: the preservation of the country.

consecrate – This doesn't mean to think really hard about something. To consecrate something means to make it sacred.

four score and seven – Lincoln wasn't talking about touchdowns or home runs. In this case, score means a total of 20 things. Four score means four 20s, and four 20s equals 80. Add seven more years, and you get 87. So, "four score and seven" is just a long way of saying 87.

last full measure of devotion – No need for rulers here. Lincoln meant the soldiers gave everything they had — literally — for the cause of keeping the nation together.

new birth of freedom – This birth has nothing to do with babies. Lincoln was talking about making all citizens, black and white, free.

Glossary

civil war (SIV-il WOR) — a war between different sections or parties of the same country or nation

consecrate (CON-suh-krate) — to bless or make holy

dedicate (DED-uh-kate) — to set apart for a special purpose; a dedication is a special ceremony at the opening of a new bridge, hospital, cemetery, or the like.

devotion (di-VOH-shuhn) — the act of giving your time, effort, or attention to some purpose

endure (en-DUR) — to last for a long time

engaged (en-GAYJD) — involved in doing something

hallow (HAL-oh) — to make sacred or holy

liberty (LIB-ur-tee) — freedom from restriction or control

perish (PER-ish) — to die or to be destroyed

preserve (pri-ZURV) — to protect something so that it stays in its original state

proposition (prop-uh-ZI-shuhn) — an offer or suggestion of an idea

resolve (ri-ZOLVE) — to decide that you will try hard to do something

Internet Sites

FactHound offers a safe, fun way to find Internet sites related to this book. All of the sites on FactHound have been researched by our staff.

Here's how:

1. Visit *www.facthound.com*

2. Choose your grade level.

3. Type in this book ID **1429619309** for age-appropriate sites. You may also browse subjects by clicking on letters, or by clicking on pictures and words.

4. Click on the **Fetch It** button.

FactHound will fetch the best sites for you!

Read More

Burgan, Michael. *The Battle of Gettysburg.* Graphic History. Mankato, Minn.: Capstone Press, 2006.

Hansen, Sarah. *Abraham Lincoln.* Presidents of the U.S.A. Mankato, Minn.: Child's World, 2008.

Olson, Steven P. *Lincoln's Gettysburg Address.* Great Historic Debates and Speeches. New York: Rosen, 2005.

Price Hossell, Karen. *The Gettysburg Address.* Voices of Freedom. Chicago: Heinemann, 2006.

Index